# Rise

## A CHILD'S GUIDE TO EASTERTIDE

Laura Alary

Illustrated by Giuliano Ferri

PARACLETE PRESS
BREWSTER, MASSACHUSETTS

This is the season of Easter.
The church is dressed in white and gold.

The world outside has its own seasons
and its own colors.

White and gold are here too,
in snowdrops and daffodils,
forsythia and dandelions,
clouds and sunshine.

Pink and purple blossom on branches.
Held in the hollow of a tiny nest,
sky-blue eggs wait to hatch.

The world is coming alive again.

# In the Garden

*It is still dark as Mary walks*
*along the winding path.*
*Ancient trees cast spooky shadows.*
*Mary shivers.*

*Only days ago*
*she sat with Jesus around a table,*
*sharing food and stories.*
*When he passed her the bread,*
*his hands were warm.*
*But now he is dead.*
*His body lies in a tomb*
*in this old garden.*

*Mary has come*
*to wash and wrap him,*
*the way family do for those they love.*

But when she reaches the tomb,
its mouth yawns dark and empty.
Jesus is gone.

Where? Why? How?
Who has taken him?

Mary weeps.
She is too late.
She has lost her chance
to touch Jesus one last time.

Then she hears a voice.

Someone is there in the shadows.
At first, her eyes do not know him.
But her heart tells her who it is.

Mary flings her arms around Jesus
until he whispers she can let go.
She doesn't need to hold onto him anymore.

At my church,
Easter begins in the dark.

Early in the morning
we go to the lake
to watch the sun rise.

As the sky changes,
we hear how God made Jesus alive again.
We greet each other in a special way:

*Christ is risen!*
*The Lord is risen indeed!*

Later we go back to our big church.
It is bright with flowers and
colors and music.
Our words and songs are
full of *hallelujahs*.

Easter is a joyful day.
But there is a bit of sadness in it too.
Jesus came back to Mary.
I wish the ones I love
would come back to me.

My nana told me
that when living things die
they go back to the earth
and help new things grow.

I wonder if they are gone.
Or changed into something else.

One day we found a caterpillar.
It crawled onto a twig
and made itself a sleeping bag called a chrysalis.
Inside that chrysalis,
its body changed.

When the butterfly broke out,
Nana told me not to touch it
or it would not be able to fly.
Its wings were damp and crumpled.
After drying them in the sun,
the butterfly rose up on a breeze.

I wonder why Jesus told Mary
not to hold onto him.
Maybe he was changed too.
Maybe he wanted her to know
it was okay to let go.
He would be with her
in a new way.

# At the Table

*The sun is high in the sky*
*as two friends trudge along the road.*
*Behind them is the city of Jerusalem,*
*they are not sure what lies ahead.*

*Only a week ago,*
*they walked this road with Jesus.*
*Everything was different then.*
*They were headed toward the city,*
*full of songs and hope.*
*Now no one feels like singing.*
*Jesus is dead.*

*Or is he?*

*This very morning,*
*Mary came running,*
*breathless with news:*
*I have seen Jesus!*

*They want to believe it.*
*But wanting does not make it true.*
*As they walk and wonder, a stranger joins them.*

*He wants to know more, so they tell him about Jesus,*
*things he said and did, things they hoped he would do.*

*Then the stranger tells stories of his own—*
*familiar ones about Moses*
*and the prophets, but with a twist.*

*The friends are amazed.*
*How is it that these old stories*
*now make them think of Jesus?*

*It seems like he has been hiding*
*in the words,*
*waiting for them to find him.*

*When it is time for supper,*
*they hold onto the stranger*
*and beg him to stay.*

*At the table,*
*the stranger takes bread,*
*gives thanks to God,*
*breaks the loaf,*
*and gives it to them.*

*Then, in the blink of an eye, he is gone.*

*Or is he?*

*Wide-eyed, they stare at his empty place.*
*They can no longer see him,*
*but their hearts tell them*
*he is still with them:*

*In stories.*
*In bread and wine.*
*In friends around a table.*

On the first Sunday of Easter
we have a big dinner.
Our table is crowded
with food and people.

My nana brings her special casserole.
It was my Grandpa's favorite.
The taste makes me think of him.

Grandpa died last year.
I miss him.
His empty place feels wrong.
But I can feel him with us
in the food we share
and the stories we tell.

Easter Sunday is a big day,
but this is only the beginning.
Easter lasts for a whole season! Fifty days!
We call this time Eastertide.

During Eastertide
we hear stories about Jesus
after God made him alive again.
He is changed—not the same as before.
He comes and goes,
appears and disappears.

It seems like Jesus
is playing hide-and-seek,
making his friends look for him,
until they can see him everywhere.

# On the Beach

*Early one morning,*
*in a small boat on a dark sea,*
*Peter and his friends are fishing.*
*They have been out for hours,*
*but their nets are still empty.*

*Peter blames himself.*
*Nothing has gone right*
*since that terrible night*
*when the soldiers came for Jesus.*
*Peter was so afraid,*
*he ran away and left Jesus alone.*
*Even worse, he swore—*
*once, twice, three times—*
*that Jesus was no friend of his!*

*Now it is too late to say sorry.*

*Then Peter hears a voice,*
*calling across the water: Let down your nets!*
*When they haul them in again,*
*the nets are filled to bursting.*

*Wide-eyed, Peter and his friends*
*strain to see in the early morning light.*
*They can barely make out*
*the shadowy figure on the beach.*
*But their hearts tell them who it is.*

*The others start to row,*
*but Peter can't wait.*
*He leaps into the water and swims.*

*When they reach the shore,*
*they are welcomed by a driftwood fire,*
*soft, fresh bread,*
*and steaming fish.*
*It feels so good to be fed.*

*After breakfast,*
*Jesus calls Peter to follow him.*
*As they walk along the beach,*
*once, twice, three times,*
*Jesus asks Peter: Do you love me?*
*Once, twice, three times,*
*Peter says: yes.*

*Then Jesus looks at Peter with love.*
*"Take care of my sheep," he says.*

*A change comes over Peter.*
*He feels so happy he could dance.*
*So light he could rise up and soar like a bird.*
*He is ready to begin again.*

*Resurrection* is a big word.
It means *rise again*.
I used to think it was a word
only for what happened to Jesus.
But now I'm not so sure.

Sometimes we all trip and fall.
But falling does not have to be
the end of the story.

Jesus' friend Peter did something bad
because he was scared.
But Jesus let him try again.

I like how Jesus feeds his friends,
even if they didn't really deserve it.
I like how he gives Peter another chance
to show what he can do.
Maybe Jesus could see
that Peter was much more
than the mistake he made.

Maybe this is resurrection too.

# In Everything

*Before he died,*
*but when he knew*
*it was almost time*
*for him to go,*
*Jesus called his friends*
*to share a meal.*

*They were brimming with questions:*

*Where are you going?*
*How will we follow you?*
*When will we see you again?*

*Jesus answered them with word-pictures:*

*I am the good shepherd*
*who leads the way to food and rest.*
*I am the host who sets the table*
*and fills your plate and cup.*

*I am the vine and you are the branches.*
*Life flows through me to you so fruit can grow.*
*That fruit is love.*

*If you want to find me,*
*look for these things.*

*Look for hungry ones being fed.*
*Look for lonely ones being welcomed.*
*Look for new life sprouting.*
*Look for love at work.*

*When you see them,*
*you are seeing me,*
*and the One who sent me.*

During Eastertide we look
for signs of new life.

Some robins built a nest near our mailbox
and now the eggs have hatched.
I like how the baby birds open their mouths so wide.
They know their mama will feed them.

We walk in the woods,
and eat our lunch by a tree.
Underneath us, in the soil,
trees are having a picnic of their own.
Long threads of fungus connect their roots,
so they can send messages and share food.

They look after each other
in their own way.

We go to a farm
to see baby lambs.
One can hardly stand up
on his wobbly legs.
I call him Peter
because he keeps falling down
and getting up again.

Love is all around us.

Once a month my church has a dinner
for anyone who wants a meal.
Some people come for the food.
Others for the company.
We make special Easter bread and bring it to share.

I help set the tables and serve the meal.
I can be a host and shepherd too.
I wonder if people can see Jesus in me.

On weekends we help our neighbors
clean up their yards for spring.
There are a lot of dandelions.
We let them grow.
They are so pretty,
and good food for bees.

Nana told me a secret about dandelions.
The yellow flowers are the sun,
the fluffy gray globes are the moon,
and—when you blow on them—the seeds are stars.

I like that I can see such big things
in a little flower.

# Easter People

Sometimes little things help us see big things.
Like the sun and moon and stars in a dandelion.
Like Jesus in the bread.

Easter is like that too.
It is a big celebration—fifty days!
But it helps us see something even bigger.
Easter is for everyone.
And it is *all the time.*

I used to wonder
what the story had to do with me.
But now I see.

When we let go of things—even our own mistakes,
when we look for Jesus and find him in new places,
when we fall and get up again,
when we share a feast,
when we love—
that is Easter.

We are Easter people.

To my parents, Lynne and Murray Alary,
who helped me up after many falls.

*—L.A.*

2025 First Printing
*Rise: A Child's Guide to Eastertide*

ISBN 978-1-64060-888-7



Library of Congress Cataloging-in-Publication Data
Names: Alary, Laura, author. | Ferri, Giuliano, illustrator.
Title: Rise: a child's guide to Eastertide / Laura Alary ; illustrated by Giuliano Ferri.
Description: Brewster, Massachusetts : Paraclete Press, [2025] | Audience: Ages 4-8 | Summary: "Two children discover all the exciting themes and rituals of Easter. There is a beautiful conversation between historical flashbacks and modern-day connections"– Provided by publisher.
Identifiers: LCCN 2024018618 (print) | LCCN 2024018619 (ebook) | ISBN 9781640608887 (tradepaper) | ISBN 9781640608900 (pdf) | ISBN 9781640608894 (epub)
Subjects: LCSH: Easter–Juvenile literature. | Jesus Christ–Resurrection–Juvenile literature.
Classification: LCC BV55 .A39 2025 (print) | LCC BV55 (ebook) | DDC 232.9/7–dc23/eng/20240513
LC record available at https://lccn.loc.gov/2024018618
LC ebook record available at https://lccn.loc.gov/2024018619
10 9 8 7 6 5 4 3 2 1



Cover design: Paraclete Design
Cover art: Giuliano Ferri

Published by Paraclete Press
Brewster, Massachusetts
www.paracletepress.com

Manufactured by: RR DONNELLEY (GUANGDONG PRINTING SOLUTIONS CO.,LTD)
Printed August 2024, in Dongguan, Guangdong, China
Batch #: 20240827GPSL